YES YOU CAN SERIES

CONTROL AND INFLUENCE OTHERS THROUGH THE INCREDIBLE SECRET POWER OF ORDINARY SPEECH

SUPERNATURAL WORDS OF POWER

MARIA D' ANDREA

YES YOU CAN SERIES

SUPERNATURAL WORDS OF POWER

CONTROL AND INFLUENCE OTHERS
THROUGH THE INCREDIBLE SECRET
POWER OF ORDINARY SPEECH

By Maria D'Andrea, MsD, D.D., DRH

INNER LIGHT/GLOBAL COMMUNICATIONS

YES YOU CAN SERIES

Supernatural Words of Power

By Maria D'Andrea, MsD, D.D., DRH

Published by Timothy Green Beckley

DBA Inner Light/Global Communications - All Rights Reserved

Printed in the United States of America

Non-Fiction

Timothy Green Beckley: Editorial Director

Carol Ann Rodriguez: Publishers Assistant

Editor & Graphics: Tim R. Swartz

Sean Casteel: Associate Editor

William Kern: Associate Editor

Email: mrufo8@hotmail.com

www.ConspiracyJournal.Com

CONTENTS

DEDICATION

To My Family For All Their Support:

Rob D'Andrea: My son, who has a great heart, a giving nature and is always selfless.

Rick Holecek: My son, who is a great counselor, teacher of life and comes from the heart.

Gina Holecek: My daughter- in- law, who is truly a daughter, intelligent and good with people.

Ryan Holecek: My grandson, who is all heart, smart and goal oriented.

Cara Holecek: My granddaughter, who is creative, smart and loving.

FOREWORD

By Robert D'Andrea

IN her newest book, Rev. Maria D'Andrea explains to us the "*Supernatural Words of Power*" and the massive effect that they have in shaping our lives. We will learn the importance of how we phrase our thoughts, what we put out to the universe, as well as the words that we choose when we manifest. Our futures are directly affected by what we say and think, so it is of the utmost importance to learn how we can choose the best words and phrases.

After reading her newest book I am paying close attention to my words and thoughts. I have already attracted a new friend who is extremely spiritual and I believe that we will improve the quality of living for each other. Life feels better because I am noticing more supernatural occurrences, no matter how small they may be, more often now, and I can just sense that I am on the right track.

We all need to continue learning to make our lives the best that we can because, after all, we deserve to, and Rev. Maria D'Andrea's books continue to help me do just that. I can't wait to see what the next book will teach me!!!

SUPERNATURAL IS NATURAL

WHAT does that really mean? For some reason, people think we can't work with supernatural levels because they don't understand what it is and think it's out of their reach. Yet we do things on that level all the time and don't realize or connect it to that word.

When you have an uneasy feeling around someone you just met and they didn't give you a logical or emotional reason, you are reacting from survival/supernatural instincts. You are picking up "supernaturally" that this is not a good connection for you.

So, let us look at what the real meaning pertains to.

Supernatural refers to anything outside of our normal five physical senses. These occurrences can't be explained by today's scientific outlook or measurements and aren't as common.

These are situations that the general public wouldn't understand because of the occurrences being sporadic.

These occurrences/energies have been known and consciously utilized for centuries by us as occultists (sometimes called magicians), shamans, spiritual

leaders, wizards, light workers and psychics, among other spiritually in-tune people.

We, who work with the natural, esoteric Laws and knowledge, look at it as energy frequencies that we can tune into consciously to work with them.

These energies are under the Will of all mankind. We are creators, whether it is on a conscious or subconscious level. We can harness the energies consciously to create a better life. We rule.

Sometimes they may refer to the supernatural as supernormal or psychic abilities when looked at as beyond the range of our physical senses.

We have all heard of how, as an example, a child might be caught inside a car at an accident and the father lifted the car to get the child out. Obviously, not a "natural" occurrence, right? Nonetheless, we are able to do so much more than the masses realize.

A client story:

There was a lady who said she always gets a headache. Well, the universe supplies whatever you put out in the Word, verbally or mentally. So, of course, she always had one. When she didn't, she still expected one. The universe said, 'Oh, oh, I forgot to give her one yesterday so I better give her one now...' Some people would consider that as supernatural since there isn't a medical cause that can be shown physically. Usually the medical field is baffled about the cause so they are unable to help.

So, now we come to the POWER OF THE WORD...

These Supernatural Words of Power have been consciously utilized since man could speak and even before that when man could only visualize a goal.

All cultures throughout time have utilized this ability and always will. Some used it for good, some not so much. We only do positive, *always*... I truly believe everything you do, good, bad or indifferent, eventually comes back to you. You only want the good, right?

The Power of the Word can create whatever you are manifesting into your life. As long as it is in a positive way (we hurt no one), you can achieve whatever you put your focus/intent on with will power, among other spiritual manifesting "tools." We will go over how you can create through supernatural power words a little later.

As occultists, we are very aware of what we put out verbally or in thought. Now, I don't know about you, but being human, I have negative thoughts. But as soon as I'm aware of them, I use the word "*cancel*" so I don't accidentally create that and then replace it with an opposite positive thought.

Of course, that doesn't mean that I believe the thought, just that I'm creating positive situations.

If I have a bad day or if someone does something hurtful to me, I may not wish them well at that particular moment, but I quickly replace it with "*cancel*" and thinking I wish them well or I bless them.

I may not mean it, but I'm not hurting them. Some days I'm saying "Cancel, cancel, cancel" .... and I bless everybody.... Don't you have those days?

These Words with Power are a focal point to bring about your goal. The focal point helps you to narrow your attention and to stay on track with oneness to be able to work on an altered state of mind.

Your determination and focused attention when you are speaking the Words will tune out the physical vibrations around you, the world, so that you are able to flow with the energies to create your intent.

A good way to get better at focusing is to do the following:

EXERCISE

1- Focus on the flame of a candle as long as you are comfortable. Pay attention to each tiny detail. The color and the colors within the color. The movement of the flame – directions – right, left, forward, backward, high, low, the aura surrounding the flame and so forth.

2- Do you "hear" any sounds it might make? Sizzle or something else or nothing?

3- Do you "see" any pictures inside the flame? (As in watching clouds)

4- When you feel you've done as much as you can, put the flame out and walk away.

5- Give it some time and come back to it. Light the candle once again.

6- Now, look at the candle flame and see how much you remember and you'll find you will notice a few more things than the last time.

7- I suggest you do this with a few different objects. You can do it in your office with a pen or at home with any item, a part of your car such as the wheel, anything will do.

8- Do more than one object to get better at it, but only one object at a time.

Some Words bring about more harmony and balance; some are for relationships of all types (romantic, family, parents, children, friends, neighbors, and pets), health, finances, success, luck and so on.

There are what we call "*Lost Words.*" These are words that have the ability of using frequencies to unblock the "hold pattern" in someone's body that is sick. The body will then balance itself out to be healthier.

As you can see, the Power Words are for unlimited spiritual work.

You may decide to be a lone worker or to be a group worker. It might depend on your abilities compared to those around you, or simply that you do better and focus more – as well as that you like it better – to work on your own. At times, you may decide to work one way and next time another. There

are no set rules; just what you feel is right for that particular situation. You always go by what you feel is right for you. Do not let others take power from you by influencing you in how you should work. YOU are the only one that knows. Trust yourself.

You will find this Supernatural Power of Words to be everywhere culturally when you start paying more attention. Remember, some are used consciously, some subconsciously.

A Client Story:

For instance, I had a wonderful, sweet lady client. Every time someone said she was invited to a "party" (trigger words for her), she would ultimately get very sick to her stomach physically. Now, she really had a bad time of it and did everything she could, including going to doctors, to get rid of it.

Her husband felt very bad for her and stayed with her to help. She told him she didn't have any problems with him going since all she was going to do was try to sleep. She truly didn't mind and felt bad she was keeping him from their friends and having a nice time.

We talked it over with her and her husband. The next time they were invited to a "party," he simply said does she want to go and see their friends and "hang out." She didn't even think about it before she said yes. They had a wonderful time and over the course of a few more visits to friends, she stopped reacting to the word "party." It triggered a very bad time at a party as a child. Subconsciously she reacted on a physical level, so it prevented her from going and therefore she

felt safe staying at home. Words can have negative control if we don't deal with them correctly.

There are doors for us to open and there are also ones to close.

It doesn't matter where you are in your life right now, what matters is where you will be in the future. You can create a better one by consciously being aware of your thoughts and words and keeping vigilance over them. You will be amazed how a *'little word'* change can have so much impact in your life so it can change for the better NOW.

I remember saying to one of my students that you can never change your past. You can learn and grow from it but not change it. You can look at the present and initiate your future. Start today, not tomorrow. If you normally think – I can't do _?__ change it to I CAN do ?____ and you will see a change. Expect it, knowing it is cosmic Law in action.

The universal Laws never change. It is the knowing of how to work with them that can change your life. It can turn it upside down in a positive way or in a negative, depending on your consistent thoughts.

If you are ready to improve your life, take the time to look at what needs to be changed in your thought pattern to create improvement.

Now, I know you're thinking, 'OK, I'll get to that later. I don't have enough time right now.' So, let me see.... You want a better life, but not yet? Because that's what that really means.

In which case, think first about what is scaring you. It is valid that you may have something from your past blocking you. If all you heard as a child was how you aren't smart enough, your IQ can be off the charts, but you won't use it, because you think you can't.

We are going to turn your life around. YAY! Get excited because there's a whole new wonderful world about to open up for YOU.

MAGICK IN YOU

THERE is magick in all of us. This is a time of awakening your consciousness for those who are ready. Magick is using your Supernatural Powers and Spiritual Powers to create changes in events and situations. You are on your way to a higher level of evolution.

Mankind has the free will to make these changes. Magick works on frequency changes to the astral, ethereal worlds and other dimensional planes of existence besides ours. Everything is made up of energy and we can consciously affect that energy to achieve our goals.

WARNING

This is NOT a game. It is life-changing. This transcends the mundane world. It can be dangerous, depending on what your goals are.

We ONLY work on the positive side. We need both positive and negative energies for balance, but that is a different situation. Karma is very real and you need to take it into serious consideration. Whatever you create has to be positive. We hurt none. Karma states, very

simply, that whatever you do comes back to you. You only want the positive, so only put that out.

If you have a boss that's very mean, negative and less knowledgeable then you and you want his/her job, then do so in a positive way.

Instead of thinking (Word) how they are and you want that job, focus on the person moving to a better job happily and prosperously.

You don't want to get the job because your boss got fired or hurt.

You move them in a positive way and then you can have that job. It is good and prosperous for everyone concerned. Remember, if it is great for the boss, he/she will take the job to better his/her life and those around him/her. You achieved your intent and everyone was happy.

I suggest that you start with clearing your energies of all negativity which we all pick up from our surroundings and the people around us as well as when we feel negative. (We all have some negativity or we wouldn't be human. We've all had negative thoughts.)

TO GET RID OF ALL NEGATIVITY-

To Clear Yourself So You Can Work On Anything

For 3 days: Take a bath in any type of floral water. 1-2 drops of any flowery oil – rose, violet, etc. – in your bath water will make it floral water.

While you're relaxing in the bath, burn a small white candle. It can be a small birthday candle. You can substitute pink or blue. Let it burn down while you're in the tub. About 15-20 minutes. It's alright if the candle burns out first.

Affirm: I am grateful

I am calm

I get my right answers

I automatically do the right things

Everything is working well for me

Focus on surrounding yourself with white light. Then, run (visualize it happening) blue light down through your crown chakra and out through your hands and feet to bring it up to your crown chakra and down your spine to loop back up to your crown.

Your crown chakra is at the top of your head where it meets the back of your head. This is where on a baby it looks like the hair is in a circle.

Visualize yourself in a peaceful place. When the candle is finished, and the 15-20 minutes are up, take a shower and say –

All the negativity goes from me and down the drain.

After doing the ritual for 3 days, you can do any occult and psychic work.

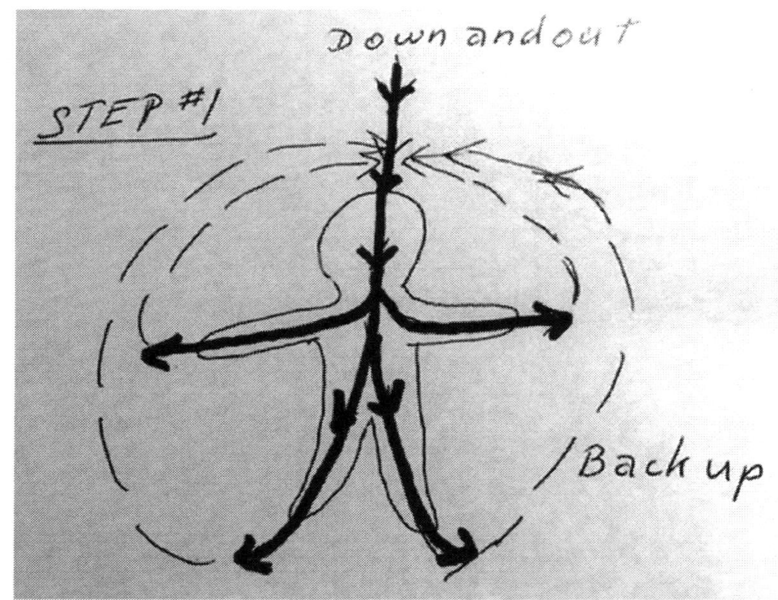
Down and out
STEP #1
Back up

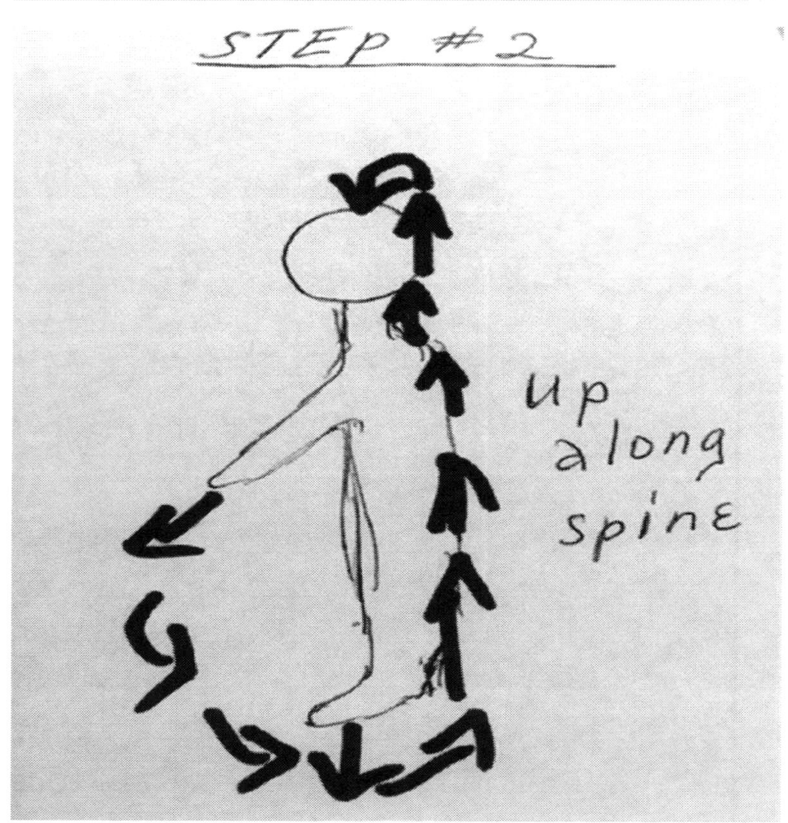
STEP #2
up
along
spine

Let it suffice that magick, in the hands of positive, knowledgeable people, can change the energies and frequencies to do good in their lives and in the world.

We are the oldest science. Everything we do is cause and effect. Science acknowledges that chemistry came out of alchemy and physics from metaphysics (magick/occult).

Occult just means ancient wisdom, hidden knowledge, not necessarily positive or negative (we as practitioners are either one or the other). It is not a religion.

Your mind and spirit working in unison are creators of your personal world. That is the real magick.

TABLES

THESE tables help add on energies to your manifesting. It is very important for you to know that they add on but are never crucially necessary in working with the Word.

When we work with Supernatural Word Power, we are going Direct. As one of my students, Rodney, aptly named it years ago –

IGD (I Go Direct)

It is like a battery charger for an extra boost.

CORRESPONDENCE OF MAGICK AND ASTROLOGY

Though it isn't necessary, perform ceremonies on the day in the hour of the correct planet. Each day and hour has its planetary ruler.

Sunday	**Ruled by the Sun**
Monday	**Ruled by the Moon**
Tuesday	**Ruled by Mars**
Wednesday	**Ruled Mercury**

Thursday	**Ruled by Jupiter**
Friday	**Ruled by Venus**
Saturday	**Ruled by Saturn**

The planet that rules the day also rules the first hour after sunrise of that same day and the hours after that are ruled by the following planets in this order:

1 - Sun

2 - Venus

3 - Mercury

4 - Moon

5 - Saturn

6 - Jupiter

7 – Mars

At sunset the hours begin again. The first hour after sunset is ruled by the planet which comes fifth in order from the planet that rules the day.

Example:

Thursday	**Friday**
(Day of Jupiter)	**(Day of Venus)**
First hour after sunrise	
Jupiter	**Venus**

Second hour after sunrise

Mars **Mercury**

Third hour after sunrise

Sun **Moon**

And so on...

First hour after sunset

Moon **Mars**

Second hour after sunset

Saturn **Moon**

Third hour after sunset

Jupiter **Venus**

And so on...

The following sunrise introduces the start of a new day. Thus each planet rules the 1st and 8th hours of the daylight and the 3rd and 10th hours of the night on its own day.

PLANETARY ACTIVITIES

Sun: Gaining favor, friends, wealth, healing, good fortune, operations concerning employers, promotions.

Moon: Love, messages, travel, emotions, medicine, dreams.

Mercury: Study, fast luck, quick money, business, divination, spiritual work, cancel of hexes.

Venus: Making friends, love, travel, fertility, art.

Mars: Energy, passion, war (offense and defense).

Jupiter: Preserving health, gaining riches, obtaining honors, legalities, court success.

Saturn: Causing good or bad fortune to business (WE only do positive), learning, destruction (again WE only do positive), gaining possessions, spiritual work for protection, legalities for family, lift negativity, protection from enemies.

Intention is really the most important factor. If the energies are there and you recognize your source as Divine Power, then nothing else matters.

Magick is a science of nature with its own laws, so to be safe, stay positive with your intentions.

Never harm anyone, as it comes back to you threefold. Threefold comes back from any work, positive or negative. Negative magick is never worth the penalty that must be paid.

Metaphysical/occult work does not have an exact time span. Some can work quickly; some may take continuous work to achieve results. After all, the pyramids didn't take a day to build either. The results were worth the wait. This does not mean we must be serious and not be joyous. Simply be aware of that which you put into motion.

PLANTING SEEDS

WE plant seeds and wait for them to mature, then we go to harvest. So it is with planting Spiritual Seeds.

We are replacing old, outdated concepts that haven't been to our benefit with new ones that will be exciting and improve our lives.

When you are putting out your thought – Word – you are planting a seed to manifest your intent.

What is in your heart and mind in connection with your spirit, even if subconsciously, will eventually manifest.

Be the Guardian at the Gate. Plant only seeds you wish to harvest later. Higher intents will garner Higher results; Lower intents will set you Low. Now, I don't know about you, but I choose the Higher Path always. You can't do better than that, right?

When you are focused on the Words, you have to be mentally clear, emotionally grounded and expect the outcome happily!!!

If you don't expect it, why would the universe bother to manifest it for you? After all, you can't want it too much....

Think of it as though your thoughts are your life, because they really are and will be.

Think first about the situation that you are changing. Be honest with yourself. Then take action.

<u>Ask yourself:</u>

1- What is the situation that I intend to change?

2- Why do I want to change it?

3- What will be better if I change it?

4- What words will change it?

5- Am I ready for the change?

6- If yes, I need to take Right Action Now, not later.

Every time you pick a Word (or Words) as a focus, consciously or not, you are manifesting. So, get your ethereal shovel and gloves and let's plant some seeds:

<u>Negative Thoughts</u>

CANCEL & TRANSFORM TO:

<u>Positive Thoughts</u>

I am unlucky

<u>I am always easily lucky</u>

SUPERNATURAL WORDS OF POWER

I am unhappy

I deserve to be happy

I hate my job

I am at peace with my job & a better situation is manifesting

My health is poor

Each day my health gets better

I don't have friends

I attract new friends who I'm happily in sync with

My life is hard

My life each day gets easier and easier

I am alone

I am connected to all of humanity & new friends come into my life now

I am fearful

I am always safe. I trust in God (put your own word) to take care of me. Love casts our all fear

I am anxious

I am the calm during the storm

I don't have any opportunities in life

I am the open door and to all opportunities

I am always stressed

My life is calm and I leave
all situations in the hands of God

I am very unhappy

I allow joy and happiness into my life

I need love

I have love when I give love

I am depressed

I can create anything in my life and I choose joy

Make up your own for the situations in your life that you are creating changes in.

Start looking at life as an adventure. It's exciting and new wonderful situations and people are coming

into your life. Give your problems up to God (or whatever you call Your Source), to take your burdens off of you and be vigilant of your thoughts and Words.

Allow yourself to grow spiritually in this process. You will raise your vibration.

Look at your life as you truly deserve to have fun, passion, excitement, success easily and effortlessly.

Begin to look at life as the Great Game of Life and you are happy and the most successful player. You Go!

SOUL PRAYER

PRAYER comes in many different forms.

I coined the name "soul prayer" because the intent comes through from your soul, not just your mental and emotional self.

Prayer is a continuous thread of words, verbal or in thought. Verbal is better when possible; it resonates stronger as a verbal vibration. Some sing it, some are solemn and some may shout. This sends a vibration into the etheric realm with force and power. The power level hinges also on the level of the focus, emotions and "knowing"/"trusting" that it works. If you don't trust it and expect it, then you will automatically tone it down in its level of effect, slow it down or even cancel it out. You can't approach this with the attitude of "let's see"...

This is a technique for calling in help from the etheric planes to aid in making your life better through creating positive changes.

Prayer can be used for protection against the darker forces, jealousy around you or any other negative energy.

There are various types of prayer to be utilized.

Such as:

Mantras

Prayer beads

Singing

Rhyming words

Chants (Such as the Gregorian chants)

Affirmation

Prayer wheels

Prayer groups

Prayer cloths/blankets

Prayer dances

Clapping/stomping to rhythm while repeating Words

Mandalas

Spoken Words or thoughts

Group sound (such as Ohm)

Incantation

Inner sound current

Intoning

And many more. I'm sure you can think of some too.

In a Prayer Power Group, as an example, there is a strong thought form built together. The same goal/intent, the same Words spoken in unison, with emotions, focus, determination, trust and expectancy. This energy goes to the etheric plane, forms and then goes to the intended goal and hits its target.

It works the same way when you are a lone Prayer Worker, Prayer Warrior or simply the spiritual power of YOU.

I remember when some of us, who use various spiritual techniques and formulae on a Higher level, got together to do prayer healing to send to a distant location for someone in need.

We put so much power and positive healing intent into it; we blew out all the lights in my house. (You know who you were in the group...) The energy was very much magnified. Even if you don't see an effect, know that the same energies are at work for you.

See which prayer fits you at various times in your life and remember that you can always make up your own. In which case: be precise, plan your Words ahead, focus your will power, trust, add your emotions to push it through and expect the outcome.

***** Remember, you can substitute whichever name you use as your Source/Deity in the following prayers.**

The prayers that are not mine will have the author's name. See which ones you resonate with for your goals.

PRAYER OF THE WARRIOR

As the river meets the ocean,

As the rising of the sun,

So shall everlasting power,

Be mine to conquer from this day on.

BLESSING

May the Great Spirit watch over you.
As long as the sun rises, the fire glows, the earth rotates and the water flows.

4 CORNERS PROTECTION PRAYER

This is a very old protection spell, updated to Christianity. Also very good for children at bed time:

There are 4 corners on my bed,

There are 4 angels at the head,

Matthew, Mark, Luke and John,

Please bless this bed that I lay on.

Amen

THE LORD IS MY SHEPHERD

Bible Psalm 23:1-4

The Lord is my shepherd; I shall not want,

He maketh me to lie down in green pastures;

He leadeth me beside the still waters;
He restoreth my soul;
He leadeth me in the path of righteousness
for his name's sake.

Yea, thou I walk through the valley
of the shadow of death,
I will fear no evil; for thou art with me;
thy rod and thy staff they comfort me.

Thou preparest a table before me in
the presence of mine enemies;
thou anointest my head with oil;
my cup runneth over,
Surely goodness and mercy shall
follow me all the days of my life:
and I will dwell in the house of the LORD forever.

FOR OTHERS

Let us pray for those in need,
For those who are sick and need to be healed,
For neighbors across this land of ours,
For countries that are far and wide,
For all to be enclosed in Light.

LOVE TRAIN

I pray that all who seek the Light,

Get on board this train tonight,

Surrounded in the Light of Love,

This train moves on from morn till night.

TRAVEL BLESSING

May God protect you on your travel and counsel you when need insight.

Show you the Path that is right for you and protect you throughout your travels far and wide.

ILLUMINATION

Divine Power, guide me so I may see the Light, understand your Truth, know inner freedom, call me to peace, take my burdens, and help me to find my inner spark of Divine Love.

So Be It.

PRAYER OF PROTECTION

By James D. Freeman

The light of God surrounds me;

The love of God enfolds me;

The power of God protects me;

The presence of God watches over me;

Wherever I am, God is!

TO AID IN LEARNING

Before you start to study, place a yellow cloth or paper underneath your study material each time. Do this prayer, then study. And when/if you are taking a test, have something near that is yellow, like a pencil (yellow sides).

Deities of air and wind,

Help me know what's needed here,

Quicker learning I now seek,

Easily and readily.

OPENNING THE SPIRITUAL DOOR

I am the door

That opens wide

Allowing Light

To come inside.

SEEKING LOVE

I am the seeker from my heart,

Searching for my Right one love,

Spirits of the Southern Realms,

Bring him/her to me I now command.

HEALING

Healing angels hear my plea,

Harness all your energies,

My heart is open to be healed,

Green, pink, blue, now it is sealed.

STRENGTH

Physical and inner strength,

Are coming to me as I am Blessed,

To help me in my endeavors now,

Through Northern energies that now abound.

AFTER A FAILURE

I have failed and I know,

That the good Lord meant it so,

To learn from it and to move on,

My Path is set now for Higher ground.

BUSINESS IMPROVEMENT

Business, business, I am ready,

To move up higher in this city,

To do better and be known,

Money flows in rivers of gold.

JOB SEARCH

East, west, north and south,

My job opportunities now abound,

Bring to me my perfect job,

I will do my best to succeed in life.

Money
Blessed
Inspiration
Happy
Confidence
Now
Uplifting
Better & Better
Success
Love
Discover
Unlimited
Give
Trust
Power
Faith
Win
Truth
Joy
Hope
Soar
Fun
Grace
Laugh
Spiritual

WORDPLAY

IF you think about it, we really are our words in numerous ways. Culturally and personally speaking.

Culturally, when you listen to people speak, you get a feeling of what it was like years ago. For instance, we say an idea hit the bull's eye/hit the target/made its mark, or the idea was "a shot in the dark" but succeeded. So we know that, at some point, people used archery, guns and other weapons.

What Words do you say frequently?

Really, think about it. Do you say, "I'm always lucky? I always get the perfect parking spot? I never miss the bus? I'm as healthy as a horse?" (Are they always healthy? Who knows? I don't have one ...but it's a positive thought)

Or do you say, "I always have a headache? I'm always tired? I never get a break?" Let's turn those words upside down (frown to a smile.) And say "cancel" and flip it to saying you are always feeling healthy. You have abundant energy. Opportunities always find you.

Remember, you don't have to believe it, although that brings in the results much faster, but you are

putting out that energy so that the changes will come over time. Depending on your focus, among other factors, it can take a few minutes or years. How much do you want the change? Where are you now? Where would you like to be?

This is where you are put to work. Yes, I said work...

1- **Make a list of all the words or thoughts you have frequently used that are not helping you be successful or are not benefitting you.**
2- **Next, put it away and come back to it on and off for seven days while you keep adding to the list or changing it.**
3- **Write your list below. Add more paper if needed. As examples:**

My Frequently Used Words

Fun

Back ache.....ETC

___

___

___

___

___

___

___

___

___

___

___

My Positive Replacement Words

Of course, keep the positive Words and keep using them. Replace the ones that do not benefit you or that fit before in your life but no longer are valid.

Fun

I feel wonderful...ETC

____

____

____

____

____

____

____

____

____

____

____

____

____

Now walk the talk....

Remind yourself when you slip up to replace the Word that you've outgrown.

It takes practice and vigilance, but it is well worth it to make a better life, don't you agree? Of course you do. After all, you are working with me and I only do positive work.

The better you do, the better those around you do. The domino effect is in play here.

Homework...yes it is...

Pay attention to those around you. Family, friends, neighbors, at the supermarket, etc. You will be amazed how their Words coincide with their lives.

And that's the end of homework... We can learn, change and still have fun.

Now, on to other Words of Power you can transform with...

CHANGE THE HURT

You can decide to change all your thoughts that hurt you to ones that can help. You are always in charge of your mind, so choose to let go of hurts and change them to: I am free of guilt, resentment, anger, hurt from others and myself.

Repeat on and off during the day - I choose to change today to freedom and joy.

I AM VICTORIOUS

You aren't a victim. You create your reality and now you are changing it to be better for you. You create what your mind focuses on. If you are worried about poverty, you will attract it, because that's what you are focused on. This also applies to any other negative situation. To create a better situation, refocus your mind/thoughts and Words, too, and repeat daily –

I am victorious. I keep my mind on sending out loving thoughts and seeing situations turning for the best. This is the only reality with (think of the person or situation you are changing).

BANISH FEAR

You can't focus on two thoughts at the same time. Do you choose love or fear? Focus your thoughts on transformation, to sending out love and feeling safe. You will experience whatever you create.

Focus your mind repeatedly on – *I choose to see the positive around me and replace fear with love. I am safe.*

JOY

Repeat daily - *I create unexpected joy in my life.*

RELATIONSHIP

It doesn't matter what type of relationship you are thinking of. It can be romantic, friendship, parent or child or even a pet.

Repeat daily – *I am non-judgmental. I am loving and so create loving, accepting relationships in my life.*

ABUNDANCE

Repeat daily - *I am the master of my life and now create abundance in all its forms.*

GIVE AND SHARE

Giving doesn't always mean money. It can be advice or anything else you may do. If you give love, you get love back. Remember the Law - Like Attracts Like.

Repeat daily – ***I am a giver and give from my heart and I accept all that comes to me with thanks.***

MISFORTUNE

All misfortune leads to growth. How will you handle it? Will you get angry and resentful and do nothing? Or will you look at the situation and see what you can learn from it, look at your options to move on and take action?

Daily repeat – ***I automatically think, say and do the right things. I am lucky and fortunate in all my dealings.***

SPIRIT TALK

Great Spirit of us all, I hear your voice in the wind, see your energies in the rainbow, feed my body from your gifts from the earth, sustain my life through the waters I drink and see in the darkness through the blaze of the flames.

I seek the knowledge of Spirit to help my loved ones, myself and all those around me. Give me the guidance to do so and the ability to know when you are guiding me.

So Be It.

LESSONS

You, Divine Power, have given me lessons in life so I can be lifted up in spirit and in abundant success.

Help me to know what Path to walk, what forks in the road of life to take.

Make me wise, loving, giving, selfless, joyful and to live in your Truth until I go home to you once again.

NATURE IS CALLING TO US

Creator of all, we know we are all connected in you.

Our energies blend with all the creatures of the earth, the Mineral Kingdom, Plant Kingdom and humankind.

We are all made up of energy and Light.

We are meant to be the guardians of Mother Earth and to work in harmony with all there is, was and shall be.

The horses let us ride them, the flowers grow more when we talk to them, and the gemstones magnetically attract positive goals to us.

Thank you for your abundant gifts. We strive to work with all in harmony until we all meet on the etheric planes.

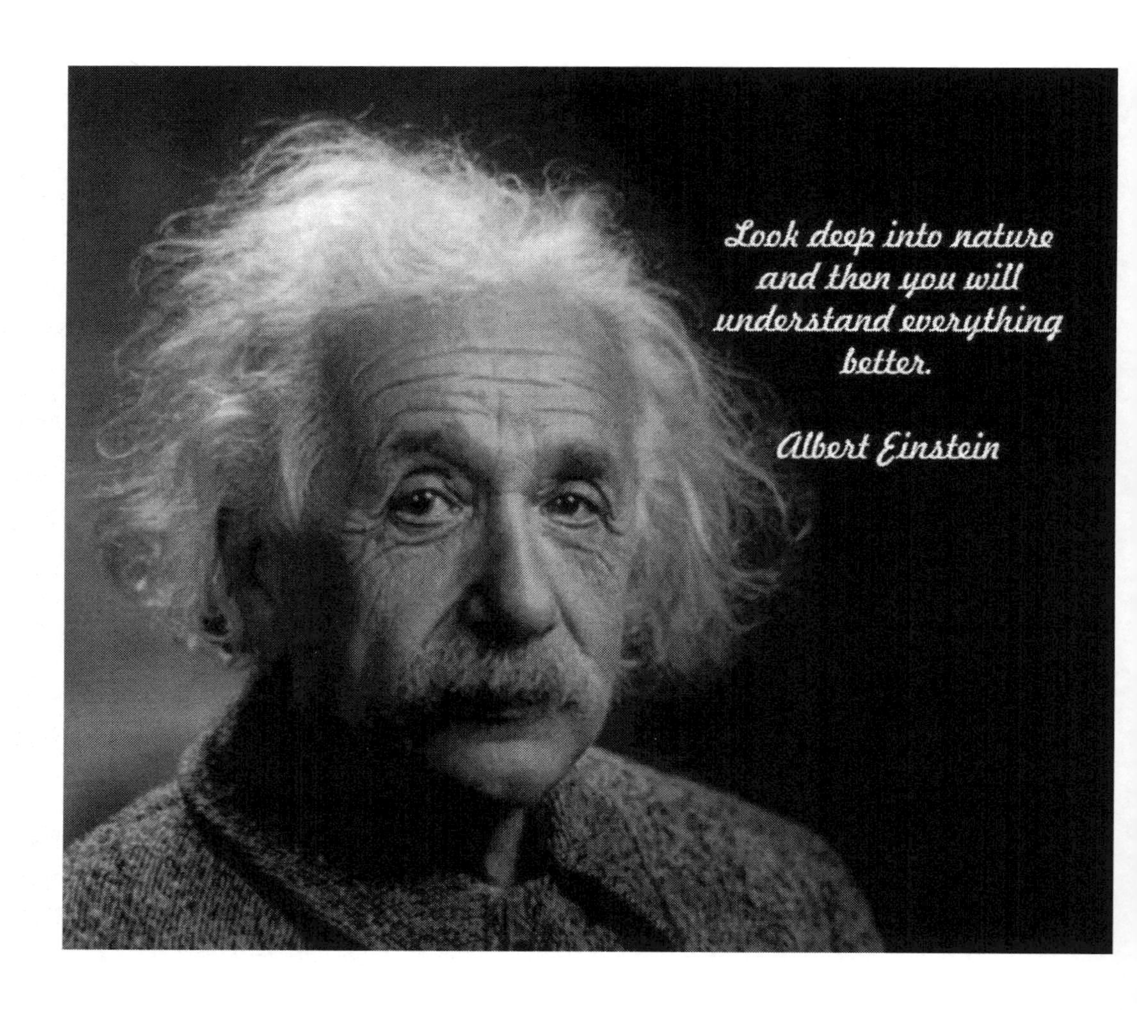
Look deep into nature
and then you will
understand everything
better.
Albert Einstein

SAYINGS

SAYINGS are part of all cultures to remind us of our failings so we can improve upon them. Our successes so we can keep them. They give us ideas on how to move on to be better or to do better.

Look at some of these sayings and pick what fits you at this time to help you to figure out what Words of Power you can utilize to improve your situation.

Some sayings are good to remember and to remind ourselves every so often to keep our thoughts in check...

If your mind

Can conceive it....

And your heart

Can believe it...

Then your hands

Will receive it...

By *A Great Soul*

To be yourself in a world that is constantly trying to make you something else is the greatest accomplishment.

By *Ralph Waldo Emerson*

Re-examine all that you have been told...
Dismiss that which insults your soul.
By *Walt Whitman*

Every day you speak your positive Word,
Your life moves higher and higher.

By Maria *D'Andrea*

Let your soul stand cool and composed before a million universes.

By *Walt Whitman*

I dwell in possibilities.

By *Emily Dickerson*

Whatever satisfies the soul is truth.

By *Walt Whitman*

(Make your dreams a reality by using your Words carefully):

All that we see or seem
is but a dream within a dream.

By *Edgar Allan Poe*

Learn from yesterday, live for today, hope for tomorrow.
The important thing is not to stop questioning.

By *Albert Einstein*

(Remember we are all equal when you confront situations):

Freedom – to walk free
and own no superior.

By *Walt Whitman*

Sayings are part of all cultures to remind us of our failings so we can improve upon them.
Our successes so we can keep them.

By *Maria D'Andrea*

Seeing, hearing, feeling, are miracles
and each part and tag of me is a miracle.

By *Walt Whitman*

The day you put out the Word,
Is the day you create your future.

By *Maria D'Andrea*

Once we believe in ourselves,
we can risk curiosity, wonder, spontaneous delight,
or any experience that reveals the human spirit.

By *E.E. Cummings*

Never lose an opportunity of seeing anything beautiful,
for beauty is God's handwriting.
By Ralph Waldo Emerson

Look deep into nature and then
you will understand everything better.

By Albert Einstein

See the Light of Truth in yourself,
Appreciate the good so you can repeat it.
And change the attributes that no longer work for you.

By *Maria D'Andrea*

YOUR FUTURE AWAITS

YOUR future is right around the corner. Go ahead, take a peek. Make it great.

So, here we are, creating our own futures and... oh, whoops... we created the wrong thing. That wasn't what we meant. We didn't want a red car, we wanted blue. We didn't want to move down the block, we wanted to move out–of–state. What do you mean I didn't get the exact job I wanted? I put out the Word...

Let's look at this in manifesting terms.

The way the universal Laws work to create are very exact in noting our thoughts or Wording. It is very technical.

To create a better world for yourself, you need the tools of knowledge about how the universe, cosmic energy, creates.

I developed this system to explain it for my students. I named it * "TAP" (c) 1970 *****

First – You form and put out your Thoughts to the Universal Energies/Divine Power.

Second – Your thoughts go to the Astral plane to form.

Third - And last, it comes down to the Physical plane to physically hit/manifest.

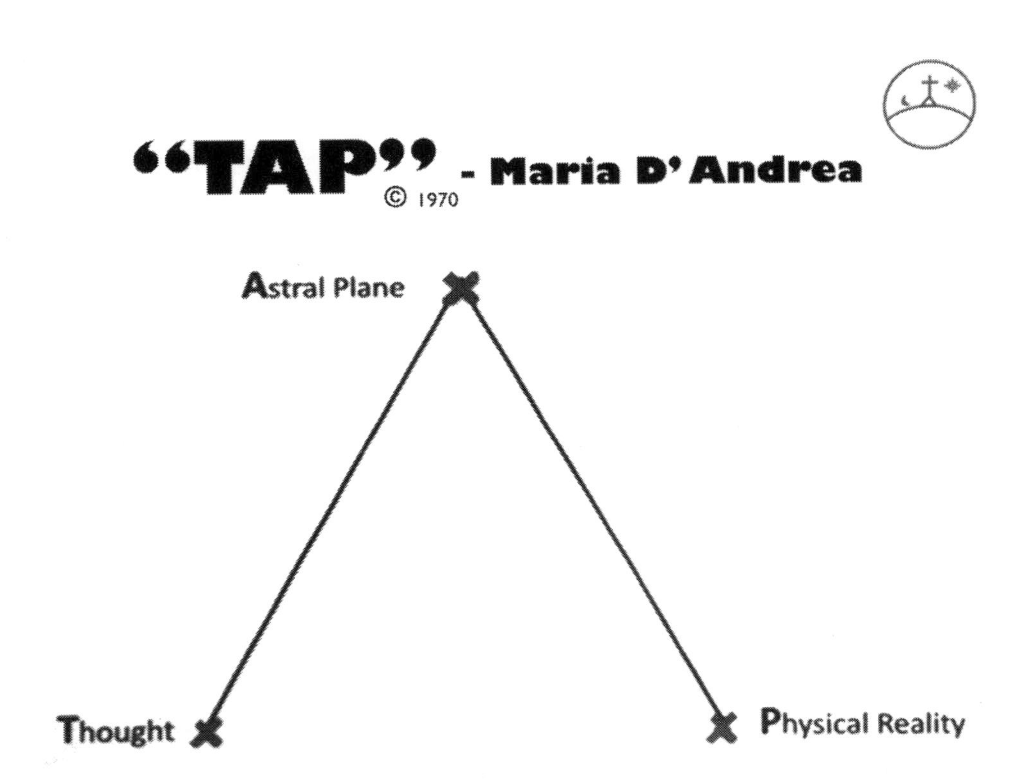

As you can see, we are very aware of our thoughts and Words at all times. At least we try to do our best. We are, after all, human.

If you have a stray or a once-in-a-while thought, it doesn't automatically mean it will manifest.

It will manifest if you are consciously putting out the Word, as I said before. Picking a goal, planning the correct Word for the situation, focusing your will power, getting your emotions behind it, sending it out with expectancy and making sure your purpose is for the good of all.

Another example is when your emotional energy is ramped up and the sheer intensity will send it out.

As an example, someone hurt you or a loved one and you are understandably very angry and obviously do not wish them well at the time. We are normal... You may wish they would get hurt to be even. Remember to use the Word "cancel." Next, replace it with the opposite and send them, in thought, "love." Now, obviously, you will not feel this love. How could you? You are a sensitive being. However, if you think it, you will not accidentally hurt them.

Remember Karmic Law – What you put out comes back.

It is sad at times that we are in these situations, but we can only control ourselves and the way we react, not others. Remember the list you made of the Words you no longer have a need for and the replacement Words? This is the time to put them to use.

Remember in this chapter at the beginning, I said as an example that you were focused on a car and it came in, but red. When what you really wanted was blue?

When you put the Word out, you have already done the other steps. Part of those were to consciously decide what you want. That means look at all the angles.

Did you just want a car that works and that you can own? Or did you want a Chevy, 4 doors, a particular year and make, in blue? Think in details. The more detailed you get, the more exact the outcome you create.

If it doesn't matter to you about the details, just that you have a nice car, then focus in that way.

The more details you think of, the longer it might take at times, but you will get the outcome you are manifesting. It is simply up to you.

Each situation is different.

Intention is also a Key. Your intent creates what will happen in your life. Think consciously about what to create. If you aren't focused on an Intention/Intent, then how do you expect the universes to know what to create for you?

What do you expect in your life? Remember, you are planting seeds for your future. Do you plan on having a bountiful harvest? Or are you inadvertently, with your Words, creating lack? Example: I don't have

the relationship I want, I don't have enough money, I'm not happy at my job, etc.

If you are perpetuating lack, CHANGE what I like to call your "mind talk." After all, you are the creator.

Hold your intent mentally, emotionally and spiritually with the following Words and check off the ones to use for yourself at this time:

____happy ____Joyful ____ excited

____ successful ____spiritual ____open

____wonderful (full of wonder) ____communicative

____playful ____ loving ____ healthy ____ inspired

___peaceful ____friendly ____fulfilled

____ambitious ____ energetic ____outgoing

____sympathetic ____free ____abundant

____intuitive ____remarkable ____valued

____inventive ____serene ____surrendering

____ releasing ____powerful ____in control

____self-accepting ____centered ____laughing

____humorous ____Divinely Guided ____strong

____magickal ____moving up ____balanced

____non-judgmental ____creative ____analytical

____Blessed ____safe ____forgiving

____understanding ____romantic ____adventurous

____trusting ____focused ____attentive

____generous ____have integrity ____supportive

____loved ____idealistic ____grounded ____growing

____aware ____protected ____beautiful/handsome

____unique ____fun ____honest

____reliable ____my Higher Self

____ADD YOUR OWN

This is the time to open doors for yourself. When you do better, so do those around you. After all, you will be in a better position to help them in some way, even if it is advice (you are growing) or a ride when they don't have a car (because you can afford a car).

Remember that you are a child of God. You have the aspects of your Father within you to use. Just like inheriting your parent's hair or eye color. How great is this? You cannot be stopped from your goals. Nobody can stand in your way. When you know God is your Father and on your side, how can you not succeed?

This is not the time to settle. This is the time to move forward. Your thoughts will turn to action.

*** Remember my system of "TAP"!!!**

When you are creating your future, don't put limitations on it. If you are manifesting a job as a manager, add the thought:

"This Or Better"

What if you don't get that particular job? You will find that you have something better that comes in. God had a better plan for you. He saw that you could do/have something better. So He gave it to you.

Client story:

I had a wonderful young man as a student who wanted to get married to his girlfriend. They were together for two years and he wanted to move forward.

Right before he had a chance to do so, she told him that she was moving out-of-state for a job. She was very happy and excited as she told him.

Obviously he was very upset and thought about how she didn't even consider discussing it with him or how he might feel. So he realized this was not the person for him and was feeling very sad about it.

Even though he didn't feel it, he put out the Word that his life is happy.

A few weeks later, he met a young lady at a coffee shop. He was carrying his coffee back to his table, not looking up, and walked into her. She had a sense of humor and laughed instead of yelling at him. They ended up having coffee together, laughing and then going out on a date. You know where this is leading,

right? I know you do.... So they were married and it was a better match for them both.

"And they lived happily ever after".... I really don't know, but it sounded good, right???

It doesn't matter where you are in your life this minute. You can always make it better, better and better. Make a conscious decision and stick to it. Don't start and the next day say to yourself: Well, I don't have the time to think about my Words today. I'm way too busy (with work, meetings, job, relationship, health, supermarket, etc.). I will continue tomorrow.

These are excuses your subconscious is giving you. Are you going to continue in the same way or are you really serious about breaking past patterns to improve your life?

Think of it as a test. If you keep going out in the rain without an umbrella and you always get drenched, wouldn't you at some point want to change that pattern and take an umbrella with you the next time? You would be changing a pattern that is not benefitting you to one that is. Same concept. Go for the umbrella.

Look at your patterns. Take your time. Do you keep going out with men/women that have the same pattern in common that isn't good for you? Such as being very critical of you instead of loving and supportive? Get out of there! Quick, run! Do you have your running shoes on? Why not? What are you getting out of it? Does it remind you of a parent or sibling or

someone else? You've outgrown it if you are reading my book. Run, run, run! You deserve better.

Remember you are a child of God and part of Him. You are a creator. Create happiness for yourself and know that God (or whoever your Source is named) is there to help you.

Learn from your past and close that door. Open the new door and step through it in Trust and happy expectation. After all, God wants you to do better, better and better.

FORGIVE AND LET GO

FORGIVENESS is crucial in letting the past go.

Also remember that it is harder to forgive yourself then to forgive others.

My bird story:

I look at it as: You have a bird and you are used to it being around you. It flies around your room. It does whatever it wants. It makes a mess everywhere and you have to clean it up. It's loud. And it bites you!

Then, one day, you leave the window open by mistake. The bird flies out. Later on, you notice your life isn't messy. Everything is in its place and you aren't feeling frustrated, unhappy and hurt.

You discover that you forgive the bird for it wasn't doing it consciously; it was simply this particular bird's basic nature (which we can't change). You let go of feeling bad about how the situation was. You are letting go and feeling better that you both moved on. So it is with our lives.

Look into yourself. Who or what situation is around you that is upsetting to you right now or in the past?

When you dwell on how someone is wronging you or has in the past, or how a situation is bad, you are holding yourself back instead of allowing yourself to move forward.

You are harming yourself. Whoever you need to forgive is not affected by your hurt or anger. That person has moved on. But you are holding on to it (sometimes because you really are in the right), but nonetheless, it slows *your* progress.

You may be feeling hurt, angry, and resentful or other feelings depending on what happened.

Look at what happened. Forgiveness does not mean you are saying what happened is alright or even that you understand. If a friend turns on you, it is *not* OK.

You are at a point where there is nothing you can do about it. It is over and in your past. If it is still going on, remember you are a being of Light and take control of the situation. Sometimes taking control means to just walk away so it doesn't keep hurting or upsetting you.

You need to stop carrying this hurt or anger around so it doesn't continue affecting you. Use your Words to let go. Remember, you are saying it was a bad situation; I can no longer do anything about it; I need to stop carrying these feelings that are slowing me down from creating my joy, happiness and freedom.

Inner freedom is spectacular. Acknowledge to yourself that you are the only one who can create your

own feelings of freedom. Then freedom will always follow. You are creating the freedom through the power of your Words/thoughts. Releasing your upsetting thoughts and hurts gives you the freedom to be happier, content, joyful and free.

We didn't change what happened; we changed your outlook to be able to create joy. Send the person/people/situation Love energy. Now, I know some of you are thinking about what happened in your life and thinking "She must be crazy" or "She must be extremely spiritual to be able to feel that." Both are wrong. Good to know, right?

This is how it really works:

You don't have to "feel" love. If someone hurts me, I am not feeling love! If I did, there would be something very wrong with me. I may still be upset as I am saying to the universe:

"I send (name of the person, people or the situation) Universal Love."

I'm only hurting myself if I'm not moving on. I admit that there were times when I spent days saying I'm sending Love to ____, I'm sending Love, I'm sending Love....

(I didn't add Grrrrrr, but, after all, we are human.)

FREEDOM EXERCISE

Repeat verbally for more vibrational power as often as needed (like taking an aspirin or herb, right?)

I am sending Love to (Name)

I forgive (name). I let go of all my negative feelings that are blocking or stopping me from moving on. I now send Universal Love energies and it SETS ME FREE!

I AM SAFE

1 - Think of Divine Power/God/Your Source as having gigantic hands that are cupped.

2 - Then visualize yourself standing with your back to these hands.

3 - Next, visualize yourself falling backward into His hands with a sense of your body becoming lighter and lighter, feeling safe and letting go.

4 - Rest there until you feel you are done. Remember, you can do this any time and as often as you chose.

SELF–FORGIVENESS

We are aware of what others have done to wrong us and so we are working on being able to forgive them so that we may move on.

We can get focused on what we've done in the past that we feel guilty about or sad or sorry for. Sometimes we look back and think, "I can't believe I did that." At times we think about how we might have hurt someone or did something bad inadvertently.

This is the time to learn from it, forgive yourself, let go and move on.

You cannot go back to what you've done. If it is something you can still fix, then move on it and do so, so that you can repair it and go forward. If it is not fixable at this point, know that from this day on, you are aware that you can only do your best.

You need to forgive yourself, because Divine Power/God/your Source already did. Sometimes you were meant to deal with certain situations in your life to learn from them. You learn from the lessons in life which are good, bad or indifferent.

If we were perfect, we wouldn't be human.

These are two methods to help you to forgive yourself:

1- **READ PSALM 25 in the Bible with focus and sincerity. Remembering that you are putting the past behind you. God loves you unconditionally and wants you to flourish, so how can you judge yourself unworthy?**

2- **THE LAW OF GRACE states that if you truly in your heart (and only you know if you mean it) look at your past and truly feel remorse and will never again repeat it, then you can call on the Law of Grace to cancel your entire negative past Karma.**

MOVE FROM NEGATIVE TO POSITIVE

WE all have situations that are not to our benefit. We might have outgrown people in our lives or situations. Sometimes that doesn't mean that a person in our life is bad or negative. It could be just that it was positive at the time but isn't any longer. We just might have grown in different directions or the person might have changed. Either way, we should move on. It is the same with situations. (Alright, sometimes it really is bad...so we have to make a change.)

***** As I always say, think of the situation as it is, use the Word "cancel" and rephrase it to its opposite, which is positive.**

The following are various other forms to utilize:

FOR COURT

Wear pink or green to court to have it go more in your favor then it would have. The shade doesn't matter. It brings out empathetic feelings toward you from those who see you, even if you don't say a word.

Never wear black or red to court, as it triggers a power play. They are power colors. Think of how judges used to wear black robes to show they are in charge. It doesn't matter if they think they are, we just want the outcome that's more in your favor.

If you are meant to go through some level of this situation for a Higher learning, than it will only work up to a point. God always has a better plan. When you look at it later, you usually see what the plan was. Stay in your knowledge that you have the "tools" spiritually to overcome and do the following:

Mentally in court, keep focused and keep repeating the words –

God is with me and puts all in my favor.

KNOW JOY

Read Psalm 126 in the Bible out loud and know that you are heard and are answered.

INSPIRATION

Be guided by your Higher Self. Repeat often:

I tap into the Source above,

To Light my way when it is dark,

Inspiration comes to me,

Through earth and air,

And fire and sea.

HEALING – SPEED UP SPELL

The Light of green surrounds me,

The Light of pink envelopes me,

The Light of God is within me,

All is healing quickly.

MOURNING

Know that even though we mourn, our loved ones are in a better place. That doesn't mean that in understanding this that we don't miss them. Being spiritual doesn't mean we look at it as they are happier so we don't miss them, or think of them less or love them less. Our mind understands but our hearts need time to heal.

With feeling say:

I am Blessed to know (think of the person's name) and I know that (name) is secure, happy and in a better place, without hardship or burdens. I now send Love and Healing energy to (name) to help in Lighting the Way.

MY MORNING PRAYER

May the sunshine bring me luck,

May the dew, drop me love,

May the earth bring money to me,

And may I live successfully.

MY EVENING PRAYER

As the setting sun goes down,

I lay my head on sacred ground,

Protected through the evening night,

Safe and secure until daylight.

PROTECTION

I ask the Lord to hold me tight,

To protect me always as my right,

From dawn to dusk,

From dusk till dawn,

My Lord protects me from it all.

NEW LOVE

Love that's new,

Now come to me,

Through fire and rain,

We're Blessed be.

NEW FRIENDSHIPS

Friendships new,

I now do seek,

That are good for me,

And good for thee.

MONEY SPELL

Money, money,

Silver and gold,

Come to me now,

And come tenfold.

NEW JOB

Hunting, hunting, I now go,

Opportunities now unfold,

My right job finds me now and so,

Success follows me wherever I go.

DEFEATING AN ENEMY

Write the name of your enemy on white paper with black ink. If you have a picture of the person, hold that also while you read Psalm 112 in the Bible.

Focus on the Psalm as you read it. Do so each day until you feel the enemy is neutralized and no longer bothers you.

Remember, we are neutralizing the negativity, yet we are not doing any harm.

VICTORY IN ALL SITUATIONS

Read Psalm 86 in the Bible with focus and expecting your victory. Know that, as you ask, it has already created the outcome in your favor. It is done.

LUCKY CLOVER

On a brown candle and a green candle, carve a four-leaf clover. Light the candles. As the flames rise, repeat with conviction:

Lucky, lucky I am to be,

From day to day,

As you shall see.

My luck is now magnetically primed,

To bring to me all luck to bind.

Let the candles burn to the socket. When done, throw away the remainder of the candles outside your home.

Look for luck everywhere. Know you are lucky in all areas of your life.

TO SOLVE A PROBLEM

Prior to going to sleep, fill a glass of water to bring by your bed.

Hold the glass between your hands as you focus on the problem at hand in as much detail as you can.

Now, drink half of the water while focusing on asking for a solution.

Go to sleep with the glass of water being within reach.

Upon awakening, drink the other half of the water.

You will get your answer in your dream state or sometime during the next day.

If needed, repeat this until you get your answer. Remember to expect it and to look for the answer. This works.

ILLUMINATION

THIS is the time to awaken your illumination within.

Take control of your life now and move forward. What are you waiting for?

Get up off of that couch and ride that train to your better life. Choo choo...!

We are serious about what we do, but you will find that the more you get into dealing with the supernatural, the more warped our humor gets, but in a good way.

Illumination comes in many guises. It can come as intuition, a gut feeling, a knowing, psychic insight, prophetic dream, through meditation, or all of a sudden you just know (awakened by a thought as if hit by lightning) or any number of ways.

You have to keep open and express an attitude of knowing it will come to you. Be positive, honest, trustworthy, loving, all the traits that show you are walking the Right Path.

There is a saying – "Walk the talk."

Whatever you think is impossible *is* possible. You can be healed no matter what others say; you can find

the right romantic relationship at 109 years old; you can start a new career at any time; and you can travel even though you don't have the money yet.

If you limit yourself by the thoughts you have, you are cancelling out your good. After all, God is unlimited. If he can create universes, don't you think that getting the right job to come to you is easier to do? Let Him help you. He is always there for you and wants your life to be better.

Why are you sabotaging yourself? If you think "I never have a good job," you are putting out to the universe that you expect to never have a good job and you won't. You are being listened to. Change your thoughts to change your situation.

I tell this true story when I Speak/Lecture publicly in my international travels:

Years ago, I was in a situation where I was broke, single and with two young sons. I was determined to have a house and to make their lives better in the process. Everyone told me I'd never have a house; I'd never come out of hitting bottom so extremely; would never be able to have a car or afford anything; and so it went. They were sad for me thinking how bad things were.

I asked them very nicely to stop talking to me out of lack. I became very focused on moving ahead, getting a house that I owned and not renting (I was in a small apartment).

I stared putting out the Word. I still kept positive, helped others when I could, and I truly "knew" in my heart that my house was on its way.

Since then, as I write this, I'm in my third house and it keeps getting better each time.

When you are faced with a negative situation or problem, you need to ask yourself, "How can I change this to the outcome I want?" Then take action. What are you willing to do to make the change?

You have the same abilities that I do. You just need to know the way to tap into them, and that is what my books are about. I'm giving you the tools to create a better life for yourself and others. Pick up your tools (such as the Word) and break that chain of bondage holding you back from your rightful place in this world.

Don't let other people's conception of what is possible or not possible affect you. They may not mean anything negative toward you and honestly wish you well. They just haven't gotten to the point of awareness that you have.

Illumination/awareness will put you a little out of sync with society. That is why we still teach underground for much of the knowledge we possess. That's why I have "The D'Andrea Institute for Esoteric Studies." I am sure that you agree with me that at the time of the Salem witch trials, it wouldn't have been a good idea to say you're clairaudient and having spirits speak to you. It's really hot on that stake!

Sometimes psychic awareness is good because you might have a feeling that a person you thought didn't like you actually does but can't express it. Sometimes it's the other way around, but then we know them to be an acquaintance, not a friend, so we handle it correctly.

Look at your goals. The bigger they are, the more motivated you will get. You achieve more when you have a gigantic goal. If you think, I want to make $20 more per month, you feel more relaxed and eventually you will get there. Now, think if your goal was $20,000 more per year. How much more you'd have to be motivated! And it's funny how your energy would pick up to cover that motivation to get you moving. Now, pick a real goal that is gigantic.

Use your imagination to set your goals. Without imagining your outcome, how can you create?

Create your goals for various areas in your life:

Fun and adventure	**Finance**
Physical activity and health	**Knowledge**
Growth	**Giving back to others**
Romantic	**Freedom**
Comfort	**Power**
Friendship	**Success**

There has to be a balance between work and fun. We need both to function happily.

Remember, with God/Source, you are unlimited. The only thing that can get in your way is *you*.

8 STEPS TO ACHIEVE YOUR GOALS

Write in your answers:

1-Decide what goal(s) you are creating into your life. Use your imagination!

2-What is the purpose of your goal?

3-How will it make your life better?

4-What changes do you have to make in your thoughts/Words?

5-What changes do you have to make with your actions?

6-What abilities do you have to achieve this?

7-What abilities do you need to improve to achieve this?

(Reading up on it, going back to school, repeating the ability you have until you have it down, etc.)

8-Where/who can help you?

Remember the following:

1-The struggles you may have to get there make you who you are and help you to appreciate it when you achieve it.

2-Focus on your goal every day for at least *three* times a day. Think of the outcome, not the process. Feel it emotionally. How will you feel once you achieve your goal?

3-IMAGINATION IS A KEY. Without imagination, you can't conceive of your goal. Even if you don't have the knowledge, but you have the vision, it will come!

4-Have patience, knowing it is manifesting in the Right way.

5-KNOW that it is being created as soon as you are starting.

6-Remember to mentally use the Word "cancel" whenever you have a doubt or when others tell you why it won't be achieved. Sometimes it's just as well not to tell others until it is manifested.

7-Repeat to yourself: No doubt, No doubt.

8-And replace it with a powerful Word or combination of words that is the opposite.

ELEMENTAL SPIRITS

First speak these words three times, and then focus on the outcome of your intent.

Through fire and air,

And earth and sea,

What I manifest,

Now comes to me.

GOOD OR BAD

Whether something is considered good or bad depends on your concept of it. If you get a creative job and you're creative, it's great. If you are very analytical and the boss wants you to be very creative, it might be a difficult job. You are simply in your wrong place.

Try to remember that you are now creating experiences that are positive for you. Not necessarily positive for someone else.

Repeat:

As I create my life to be,

I create good to enfold me,

Throughout my life,

This shall be so,

As I now command,

My goal hits home.

Speaking of goals... Goals are created by focusing your intent to realign with your new vision.

Ask yourself, why are you where you are in your life right now? Why are you living like this (positive and negative)? What thoughts from your past created this? What are your thoughts, values that created this? If you've outlived a pattern or a situation, now is the time to let it go and create a better intent through focused vision.

There are people who are afraid the changes they make will have a negative effect on their relationships, jobs or life.

That is why we look at all aspects and decide consciously on a goal.

Student's story:

One of my lovely students was very overweight. To the point that her doctor told her that if she doesn't drop the weight, she had her years of life numbered.

She was, of course, very upset. She went home and told her husband. He was very supportive because he loved her and didn't want anything to happen to her.

She never felt pretty because of her weight and she was always tired. As she started dropping weight, her energy increased and she started to feel better about herself.

However, when she first met her husband, she was overweight, and that was what he was attracted to. He wasn't attracted to thinner women. When she started to drop to a point where she was becoming thinner and thinner, he kept saying to her that, since that was enough for her health, to please stop dropping more weight. He even explained several times why he said that.

So she consciously looked at her situation. On the one hand, she felt better than she ever had in her life and was healthier; on the other hand, there was a chance of her husband leaving.

She made the decision to continue to feel healthier and be more active and to feel better about herself. She had never had any of those feelings in her life and didn't want to give them up.

Eventually, her husband left her. But her lifestyle no longer hinged around the T.V. shows on the couch with him or around the refrigerator and she had energy to do adventurous things. They had outgrown each other.

She met a man who appreciated her and also had the same mindset and eventually they were married. Her ex-husband also met a heavyset lady and remarried and was also happy. He and the formerly overweight student are still friends.

So be conscious of how your changes improve your life and how they will affect it.

We are magick workers, healers, prophets, seekers, travelers into other realms. We are the creators, not the victims. We create our lives and, if we decide we have outgrown some of it, we create through change a new reality.

We pass down the knowledge for others to have a better life. We are all One. If your life gets better, so do other people's lives around you. Yay. You helped without even trying. That feels good.

Be the Master of your own life. When you manifest your intent, you are calling in the energies of the universe to come and help you. And God/Your Source will always answer your call. I can hear all those doors opening now.

Here are some Edgar Cayce sayings, uttered while he was in a trance as the Sleeping Prophet, to help you with your intents:

...Seek, for only the seeker will find...

...He that is faithful is not given a burden beyond that he is able to bear...

...Know that there is within self all healing that may be accomplished for the body...

...The spirit does not call on anyone to live that (which) it does not already know and understand...

...Know that what is truly thine cannot be taken from thee...

You will find that it doesn't matter what your belief system is, they all say the same Truth in different ways. Truth is Truth.

SPIRIT GAVE ME "YAHONE"

IN 2012, as a shaman, I was at a drum circle and, as the drumming went on, I "heard" clairaudiently the Word "Yahone". (Pronounced as the underlined letters: Yacht –home- neighbor).

I was told how to use this Word to create.

Verbally, in your mind or in a low voice (verbal is better), repeat the Word frequently while focusing on what you are creating. Such as: all bills paid, free to travel, prosperity, specific amount of money, healing, love, ability to do whatever I want to do....

You can make this into a chant if you'd like by rhythmically repeating this Word.

Hold the vision of your intent. You will feel the urge to stop when it is time to do so. Then expect it. It is already on the way.

Set Aside Sacred Time

This step is part of the occult sciences. Thinking about your goals is not enough. Your focus and your intent/goal need to be realigned. Make sure you put time away for this. If it is important to you, you will

find the time. You may find that going to the mountains, beach, park or just to a room that makes you feel good will do it.

Make sure you don't have any distractions.

The best way is to set aside a week to focus and connect it to your vision to realign them. If you can't take that much time, and we all can't, then set aside at least an hour or so per day or week. If your intent is serious and strong then it will be enough.

Shine your Light to illuminate the world. Create and express yourself in your own ways. This is your God-given right and your Specialty.

It doesn't matter where you are right now. Amazing things can happen and are coming to you. Stay positive; you know there's still time to change the game of life. Open your mind and heart; what you are looking for is still out there. Live the life you imagined. Go create it!

This is your time to move forward and create a better life.

"Around here, however, we don't look backwards for very long. We keep moving forward, opening up new doors and doing new things, because we're curious...and curiosity keeps leading us down new paths."

By Walt Disney

Below, write one thing you are going to focus on and put your intent into to realign your life to a more positive situation.

A quote from the Bible, Joshua 2:21: *"According to your words, so be it."*

This is my Promise:

____

Your Signature:____

Copy this over and sign it. Frequently look at it. Then follow through. Your focus <u>is to read each day, as you go, seven times:</u>

Day 1: With God/my Source, nothing is impossible.

Day 2: I have faith and don't doubt.

Day 3: I am always Blessed.

Day 4: Knock and it shall be opened.

Day 5: My supply of prosperity overflows.

Day 6: Supernatural provisions are now released to me.

Day 7: Wherever I put my focus and vision is what I create.

At this point, *<u>Stop</u>* focusing and praying for what you need, for what you are missing.

Start **saying Thanks for all the surplus coming to you.**

"For as a man thinks in his heart, so is he."

Proverb 23: 7 (NKJV)

Success is already divinely yours. It is already ordained. In all belief systems, they say how we already have the tools to be successful in this, our lives. We need to listen to the Words of supernatural power and then move on them.

If you had a broken chair and someone reached out to you and gave you the tool to fix it, wouldn't you take the tool and do so? So, here I've given you the tool, go and fix....

Remember that we also give back. It is a circle. Giving back can be money, but... it can be giving someone a ride, helping with advice or any number of other things. Don't limit it to just money.

Allow your heart, mind and spirit to focus on creating the positive in your life. Think in terms of prosperity. You know it is coming. Don't block it. Nobody can keep you from your good, only you can do that. Remember that you are meant to be happy, loved, healthy, and prosperous.

When you wake up, expect, think/say:

My day will be full of joy and a surplus of prosperity. Everything I say, think and do aligns with my intents.

When you go to bed, think/say:

Thank you Lord for this day and all the glorious days to come.

The supernatural power of the Word is given to you to help you to rise, to soar above the mundane every day issues and to begin your journey to self-confidence, knowing you are on your Right Path.

Negative people and situations may come up to stop or block you from your good. It is a test... Will you KNOW that you are meant to be prosperous and free or will you slide back and let negativity pull you down? We are all living in this reality but we know that we aren't limited by it. Rise above the tests and move forward, the way you are meant to. I think of it as - it is like a little hiccup. Remember the saying - *"This too shall pass"*.

So when you feel slowed down in your progress, or negativity is raising its head, just do as I do and remind yourself – It's only a hiccup.

Then put out the Word again. What matters is what you do today and are creating for your future.

<u>I had a student:</u>

Robert was always helping others. If he had it, so did anyone else in need. It came from his heart. At the time, he was renting a basement apartment with bad conditions.

He went to work every day with a positive attitude and saved his money when he could. He started to use the Word to align his focus, intent, trust, expectation and made time for his sacred time each night. Even

when he skipped a night (life gets in the way sometimes, which is normal), he would simply continue the next time.

He knew his intent was coming to manifest. His goal was to afford a $90,000 condominium eventually when he retired.

Right before he was to retire, he came into $100,000. Not only did he have the $90,000 but more. Who would've thought? (We would, right?) You never know how it will happen. Just that it does.

Always focus on the outcome, not the process.

CONCLUSION

UNLEASH your inner power. Create! Create! Create!

Your future is in your own hands. Think of all the inner power you control. The universal energies are truly at your disposal to create a happier, better life. You are now a "*wordsmith.*"

You know the aspirations that are in your heart. God/Divine Power wants you to be happy, fulfilled and enjoying life to the fullest. This is YOUR time. Go for it. What are you waiting for?

30 DAY CHALLENGE

I am giving you a 30 Day Challenge. Note the starting and ending dates. Look at how your life is in every aspect right now. Then make the changes with your Words and, at the end of the 30 days, look at your life again. See what positive changes you created. Stay vigilant with your Words/thoughts and you will be amazed. Now, keep it up.

Change your Words, change your life!

YES YOU CAN!!!

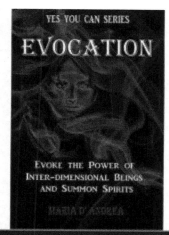

78923898R00059

Made in the USA
Columbia, SC
22 October 2017